T0082932

The Trail of Time

Victoria Sekyere

authorHOUSE®

AuthorHouse™
1663 Liberty Drive
Bloomington, IN 47403
www.authorhouse.com
Phone: 833-262-8899

Published by AuthorHouse 01/20/2022

ISBN: 978-1-6655-4980-6 (sc)
ISBN: 978-1-6655-4979-0 (e)

Contents

The untaught lesson

A wise man once said, you can love, but you must lose, but don't lose thyself through all phases of life. A lesson untaught to her was the one that took her soul. She loved, she gave until she had nothing left to offer but the shattered pieces of her broken spirit, and even then, the broken pieces weren't enough to captivate his eyes, move his heart and claim his love. She became his show, he controlled all the strings, and of course, it stings, but it was all right because that was it. The path to achieving the greatest accomplishment she has yet to see unravel. She made herself believe that his love was the beacon of light that was going to burst through her ray of sadness and uplift her spirit because a savior was all she ever really needed. His words became like acid shrouded on the whips that once broke her ancestor's flesh, and like their unmerciful oppressor, he proceeded to strip her of her dignity. The tears that streamed down her face became her closest companion. She thought of what the wise man once said, and for the first time, she saw that she had loved. She had lost, but in her last journey, she had become paralyzed. Shackled and left broken on the floor by the same love that she so desperately sought to find. Love, but you must lose, but through all phases of life, don't lose thyself.

You weren't even my type and yet
look at the damage you did

Alive yet dead.

Faded footsteps to the journey unknown.

Hollowness disguised as happiness took my heart and called it home.

Today I felt peace, yesterday I cried, and to the wise, it was blood.

Tomorrow I will laugh, and to the right set of ears, it will be the sound of the bonsho bell.

Alive yet dead.

Voice drowned in the crowd, hands a prisoner to her sides. Trapped in her mind.

Alive yet dead and to the odd set of eyes, she was what she has always been.

I would rather wander the world for centuries reminiscing of what I had than to disappear as if I never existed.

Clockwork

How is it fair?
The dead get to forget while the living breathe sentimentally
Swallowed whole, wallow and emptiness
My stomach crawled, and tears surged up my throat like acid
Burning every space that it touches.
Hold me, put me together, arrange me solemnly
Make me forget. I need to forget. All of it.
Every touch, every laugh, and all of it.
It's like a never-ending nightmare
Forgetting every night and remembering
Every morning. Like clockwork

They talked about the tragedy of your death,
to die so young, but the true tragedy is making
people love you only to leave them behind.

Hey sweetie

Have a seat next to me
Let me tell you some lessons I have learned as time went
Lessons that need to be unfolded
Lessons that have gone too long being untold
Lesson Number 1 is that Ariel wasn't that
Smart. Don't trade what makes you different
for the idealized version of a man. You will end
up as foam at the bottom of the ocean.
Lesson 2 is that princes don't kiss without permission, so
when you meet a prince that pins your arms up and tries
to take all that you are as his, don't fuss and cry. Become
a warrior with the making of fire and brim. An Alchemist
in your right. A villain if need be and reclaim yourself.
Lesson 3 is don't stand at the highest tower and wait for
the one to give motivation for an adventure. Imagine the
faraway lands entrusted to you with an ocean, the color
of the sky calling you to join it in its rhythm so you can
give praise to your maker. Press your foot so ever softly to
the ground, the color of your skin, and mold with your
fingers your imagination. Be it small or big. Run out, and
with every tired breath, live a life that you will not regret.
The last lesson you need to remember is that the beast will
always be a beast. Don't mistake it for a prince and try to
find redemption in him, or you will be eaten whole. When
it locks you in a castle with promises of a future, you only
dream of, use the strength of Samson, sewn into your hair
by your ancestors, and break away. Because you are not
meant to be stored away, you are meant to roam freely
and wild because that's when you are most beautiful.

I wish I could fly so I could touch the sky just to say I did something extraordinary.

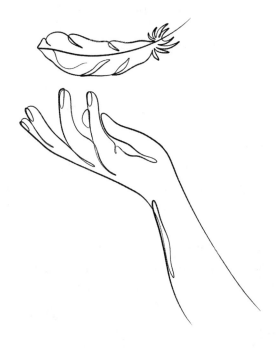

The Rise Of The King

Rise to your king
Bow to your king
Breathe for your king
Live for your king
The power of Your king is the capacity of your resilience
The will of your desires is the exchange of your liberties
So, shout loud and clear
Long live your king for how sinful it must be to breathe for
yourself
How sinful it must be to live for yourself
For what is a king without the obedience of its subjects,
And what are subjects without the demands of your king

A desire strong enough to destroy your soul
is no longer a desire but an Addiction.

Get up, I tell myself in the morning
Maybe this time it will be better
Maybe the sun will shine brighter this time
Maybe you wouldn't have to fake it all this time
Maybe you will mean your "I'm fines"
Maybe you might laugh and mean it this time
Maybe the questions will be less daunting this time
Maybe life will be gentle this time
Maybe the voices will quiet itself this time
Maybe the universe will help you out this time
Maybe all your sadness will go away this time
Because this time, I want the sun to shine brighter
Because this time, I don't have to fake it all
Because this time I mean all my "I'm fines."
Because this time, the questions bring clarity
Because this time life gave me a hug
Because this time the voices left me alone
Because this time universe lent me a hand
Because this time I'm happy
Because this time I didn't tell myself
to get up in the morning
Because this time, my soul was aware
it had finished its journey.

To be happy is to be burden free, so is it safe
to say that the dead are truly happy?

Truth

It's inevitable that all things must come to an end
Yet, the human heart is never quite prepared
for this unfortunate ending.
We yell and scream, shield our hearts with
gates of ice, but eventually, we get weary.
We release the spirit that closed our hearts, shut our eyes,
and clogged our minds, and we finally feel it. Grieve.
It hits us with the strength that loosens our teeth.
It reassures us of the failure of rising.

I never came to terms with grief. I feel the ropes tightening around my neck each day that you are not here.

The hidden desire

Do you want her? That girl? The one who walks like
she knows how precious life is. Look how beautiful she
is—surrounded by all. Tall, short, dark, and light like
she is the engineer of their happiness. Boastful laughter
crying for attention as if they are screaming. Here! Look
at me here! I find you funnier! I can make you happier!
They all have something to offer, yet she looks at you.
You wonder why? Why does the light in her eyes falter
when it lands on you? Why does she lower her head when
your presence is made known? Because she knows how
wrong it is. To love a man like you. So broken. Because
mama told her that she had picked a man that will build
a bridge, so she won't walk in the dust because Mama
said to pick a man that will build you a castle to protect
you from the rain. Because Mama said to pick a man
that protects your hands from calluses, and yet she looks
at you. A dreamer. Someone whose pain and struggles
are solemnly on his face as if announcing to the world
to give him a chance. She knows that it's wrong. So, she
continues to be surrounded by all—tall, short, dark, and
light. Boastful laughter continues—night by night.

When I asked you to hold me, I didn't mean to bind me to you. I never expected to fall in love with you, but the most hurtful part is that I never expected you to walk away from my love.

She is Me

Abandon her, they say. Leave her behind, I hear. You can't make it in life with her, but they don't understand. She is me, and I am her. She took my hands and dragged me from underneath the cross, taking my burdens as they shamed her and cast stones at her. She carried this hallowed body to the cavalry for a chance of redemption. She whispered sweet inspirations into my mouth as if she was trying to breathe a new life into me. Stroked my hair and removed my thorny crown, and when Peter, like friends, threw in the rag, she took me to the altar and made me king. She is me, and I am her. The hand that shined so brightly as she led me out of the darkness. She has been my warrior because she is me, and I am her.

I would give the world to see heaven even if it is just for a second. Just so I could see for myself that you are okay.

When I tell him that I'm sad, he asks why?
A question so simple but feels like a loaded gun pointing
at me with my back facing a cliff encompassing water.
My tongue feels heavy trying to find reasons,
but my mind writes a blank check.
I can't tell him that my head is filled with self-deprecating
thoughts undermining everything I do as regularly. I
can't tell him that I have the burden of my mother's
mother's dream on my shoulders, knocking aside anything
I deem holy. I can't tell him that I built an iron bar
around myself, painting it white, surrendering to the
words "I'm fine". I can't tell him that I get lost in my
head more than I need to because reality often becomes
hard to look in the eye, so I lie. I tell him that I'm fine.

Even if It's a lie, I need you to hold me
gently and tell me that I will be fine.

They called me a friend

held my hands and laughed
lit a candle and made an oath
some even crossed their heart
with the hope of dying, tied a knot
while whispering told secrets. I was just never aware
that one of those told secrets would one day be mine
so, when I bow upon your presence
My words become vague, and my hands
tremble with the possibility of being held
just know that I too lit a candle and took an oath
that through the rain and the rise of the sun,
I will hold my very own hand,
So, thank you for holding it until now.

The foolish idealism of friendship hurts
just a little bit more than heartbreak.

He never called me beautiful with clothes on

, so, as I lay there staring into the abyss of his eyes
wondering if I could look at his soul, he smiled,
standing over me, ready to devour
his prey. He took my hand
and pressed it to his heart as if to
remind me that he is human.
Shame rose from my stomach, wrapping its hands
around my neck, mocking me
because it knew what I knew
How much he despised me and how
much he treasured her.
He talks about her so fondly, how she
is the epitome of perfection,
elegance, and grace, but his eyes could
only find flaws in need of fixing
when he looked at me. He made me
obsessed with a woman who wasn't
aware of my existence. You see, she and I weren't all that
different. We just cried on separate pillows because, the
familiar lies that he now tells me, he rehearsed it with
her. He cages her, so she can only admire the world from
behind the bars of his so-called love while he himself did
with hands and feet. So, when he took me for the first
time with him, I saw freedom, and I never turned back,
so I write this to you, if you are to ever be freed from
your cage, run fast into the wind and just know that I'm
sorry for trying to take away what was initially yours.

I knew in the way that you held me
that he wished that it was you.

I feel blue

Maybe it's the rain outside, but I miss you.
I keep thinking of the days when all we had was a time
When we would act like rebels, smoke, and dance
you will tell me of your fears while holding me tight
too afraid that in just a second, you too will disappear
we would stay up all night creating our destiny
word by word, touch by touch, and smile by smile
A future that will never come true is all that we wished for
I don't know if our soul was aware that
we will never quite be free
as we were those days. so, wherever it
is that your destiny took you
when the clouds grace the sky, and
the first rain hit the ground
I want you to remember that I miss you.

I might have become a rebel once or twice; that was only because all I knew was how to dream.

when tomorrow comes

and I can no longer remember your face
when the sun no longer shines brightly
And your smile slowly dwindles away,
When my words can no longer reach you
and my hands keep seeking for you
when my tears keep flowing down my face
and your footstep fades
when my eyes desperately search for you
And your back blends with the crowd
just know that I tried to follow you, but an
Angel came and said, it's not my turn yet
And to rejoice, for I know that we will meet once more.

I dreamt of tomorrow, but it just never came. So, I sit idly by the window, counting down the days till we meet again.

It's okay to miss them

It's okay to reminisce about the days when
you thought they were the one.
It's okay to remember the good memories
when they held your hands and kissed your lips
when they crossed their heart and made a promise
that they will wipe your tears when it appeared
But also, it's okay to recognize the hurt
When their words no longer served its purpose
when they became the orchestra of your pain,
and humiliation, for it is not that easy to truly love.

It isn't how he loves me now that makes me stay; it is the memories of who we used to be.

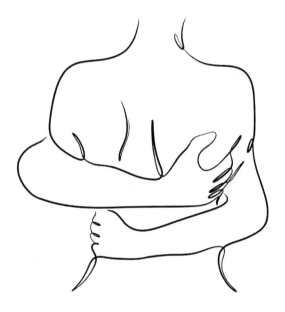

It wasn't that you didn't love me

It wasn't that I didn't love you
The truth is that you didn't see me
you didn't want to
You created an image in your head
and painted me at the center
Crucifying me to your imagination,
stripping me of all my colors
just so I could become her
and when I didn't fit
You will return home with her truth
on your tongue and her screams on your back
Simply because I just couldn't fit.

Don't cry for me

I'm not worthy of those tears
Please lift your head from the ground
For the heavens have heard your prayers
Don't let the emptiness now within
Your heart tempts you to do what I did,
Don't allow your face to be crestfallen
Like those who stand at my rest place
You see, this place was never my home and
happiness was never within my reach
so, when my father held his hand and
told me to come home, I had to leave you behind
so, when the morning dew awaken
you from your incubus, and the
early birds sing to you, their condolences.
Please do well to remember,
that I'm back at my father's home.

when I'm born again

I want the heavens to weave me
with metal and fire,
I want my skin to be molded
with the ashes of Eve and my hair
to be infused with the fallen
blood of Samson.
I want my eyes to resemble that of
Ruth and my lips to spill truth, the likes
of Delilah.
I want my body to be covered like
the armor of Goliath and for my reach to
be like David. I want my feet to walk
in troubles time the way Peter did on water
and when life gets harder, I want the redemption of Paul

I don't want to be twenty-eight

And be filled with regret, thinking
of the words I couldn't say
as you laid there running out of breath.
counting back to the days I left you, thinking
that somehow, I could make it up to you,
throwing up quarters and making wishes
somehow didn't seem to reflect
the memories I pushed aside because it caused
too much hurt, so I continue to watch until
you let out your last breath.

Have you ever been to war?

I have been to many wars
My war wasn't with things with a soul
One that could bear anger, but it was
eyes that will hold. It was with a darkness that
stayed longer, and warmth that never lasted.
It was with drinks that made me swoon, and
quite often made want to reach for the moon
It was with entities that exchanged truths for
bloody deals often draped in white resembling
a holy knight. My war was with a troubled mind
that remained awake throughout the night
craving for a drug that would give her a cause
and so, when I close my eyes and my war
comes to incite, just know that I've
Already given it my all

I used to like Blue

Blue was firm with
hands like you. Blue
will hold me tight and kiss
my lips. Blue was hard
with chest-like armor.
It will wrap me up and
swallow my sorrow. Then
I met pink. Pink is soft
with lips like cherry.
Pink was slim and so fragile
its laugh was darling
like it could call for sirens.
Pink drew me in and made
me feel whole, so when
pink left, I followed.

My friends use to ask me why I stayed

Why I traded pieces of my dignity and soul
In exchange for an illusion, I myself created.
When questions like that are asked I have no
Choice but to stay silent because words enough
Can't seem to grasp my desperation. I want to
Tell them that I thought that if I stayed on the other
line long enough he would recognize that my hand
Was held out and I was worth loving. I wanted
To tell them that I've never had any resemblance
Of love so when he smiled and took my hand
I thought the universe was trying to make up for it.
I wanted to tell them that when I heard the first
Lie come so easily out of his mouth, it sounded
Like a love song, the second one was a poem
And the third lie was like a novel. I wanted to let
Them know that it was his essence of complexity
And mischief that made him worth reading and with
a curiosity of a feline, I came to the resolution that I
Was no mystery solver. That the effort that I put in
Trying to figure him out was wasted because there
Was truly nothing to find. I stayed because I came
To the realization that he was just as empty as I was.

My mother's smile

My mother's smile is arrangeable
It hides years of retribution
yet to be avenged.
It holds wisdom and disappointment
Years of regret and a little bit of hope
hope for the better future
Hope that those who don't care will care
Hope only a mother can have
My mother's smile is one that holds pain
The pain of each generation
she procreates.
Pain that she hadn't done enough
pain that stems only from a dream of a
better outcome
within my mother's smile holds three sons
One who didn't try enough
One who was always a little late
And one that let the world slip from between their hands
within my mother's smile is a prayer
A whisper for a do-over
To right her wrongs
And rewrite her history
Within my mother's smile is failure
Failure of a dream come true.

I hold two barrels on my shoulder

One of containing dreams and possibilities and
another carries history. I was told to leave one behind
yet I simply cannot leave one or the other.
The one that holds dreams is enchanting. Promising me
things that I only dare wish for. It invites me on a journey
That my feet could barely take me
but the one that holds history
is filled with obligations. Familial obligations that bind
me in place swearing faithfulness to my pain and the
treacherous path that I have led. To leave one behind
is to forget all that it contains. So, despite its heaviness
I will continue to hold the two barrels
that sit on my shoulders
walking steadily through life, with my head high.

I always believe that I will be ruined by love

That the mere attraction of it will be my downfall
Yet as I begin to chase time and, the earth seems more
stable to walk on, I discovered that it simply wasn't true
My ruins began with familial obligations.
It was refilling a half-empty jug that
will never quite be filled.
It was picking up broken promises and trust off the floor
So, I can keep my mother's back straight.
It was trying to maintain peace while deep inside
I couldn't help but crumble. Someone told me that was
the curse of the firstborn daughter in a half-way home.
I was told that responsibilities came with my birthright,
yet I look at those made before me, and they seem so free.
They shine brighter than I do. is it because they are men?
or is it because I bear their burden now? did they
do something I couldn't do? I heard they cast their
birthright aside but if I was to do that, then what would
become of me? Would I become another tear that my
mother will have to cry? Another regret that she will
have to live with. The truth is I can't escape even if
I had the opportunity. It's become my makings.

Stay

Just stay this time
I'm not asking you to shelter me
my pain, I alone will deal
My heart too I will fix
You don't have to be my warrior
the battle will fight itself
My hand you don't need to hold
and my burdens I will bear
My tears will dry
and the parts that you hate will die
so Please stay
don't let me look back and you are of no more
don't let my mind dream of your laugh
let my ear hear its melody
Let my lips sing your chorus
Let my hands feel your warmth
so Please stay
the nights are longer
the bodies get colder
and the faces fade together
so Please stay
the birds have sung
and the trees have grown weary
the earth has bowed
so don't make me lonelier
please stay.

See you later

is a lonely word.
it holds promise
that might not be delivered
ensures hope that just might not be
and yet we just accept it.
Almost as if we are accepting the
possible failures of it.
we say it daily to those we love
because deep inside we
actually, believe that we will
make it happen.
Have you ever thought about
those who never deliver that promise?
How they create broken people
who walk around making the
same promise in hope to
fulfill that which was failed to them.
To say see you later is a cruel faith
That I can't cast on anyone
so, I will just bind you with a goodbye.

Acknowledgment

Greatest thank you to Abigail Ankomah for believing that my poems and my story were interesting to share with the public. Thank you for hunting down people who will help create my story. Thank you to Akoto for listening to me for hours so I can read each poem I wrote to him. Thank you to Akua for showing love and excitement for me. Ultimate Thanks to Danrocket Owusu For being my unofficial editor. Thanks for reading each poem over and over and for your feedback. My greatest Thank You is to those I never got the chance to say goodbye to. Thank you to my father Kingsley Asamoah for giving me the strength all these years and being the Anchor in my life. Rest in peace and I hope to meet you one day. Thank You to Prince for being a great brother to me. I'm sorry I never got to see you until you passed on. Your mother and your siblings miss you and I hope that we can meet once more. Rest in peace. Greatest Thank you is to my mother Grace Adu for always having faith in me. Thank you for cheering me on the best you can. I hope that this is the start of making me proud.

Printed in the United States
by Baker & Taylor Publisher Services